Basics

flattened crimp
1 Hold the crimp bead using the tip of your chainnose pliers. Squeeze the pliers firmly to flatten the crimp. Tug the clasp to make sure the crimp has a solid grip on the wire. If the wire slides, remove the crimp bead and repeat the steps with a new crimp bead.
2 Test that the flattened crimp is secure.

 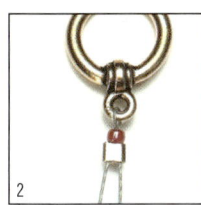

folded crimp
1 Position the crimp bead in the notch closest to the crimping pliers' handle.
2 Separate the wires and firmly squeeze the crimp.

3 Move the crimp into the notch at the pliers' tip and hold the crimp as shown. Squeeze the crimp bead, folding it in half at the indentation.
4 Test that the folded crimp is secure.

 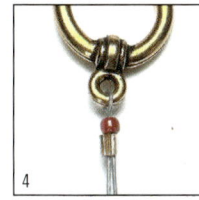

macramé square knot
1 Cross the right-hand knotting cord (rh) over the core and the left-hand knotting cord (lh) under the core.

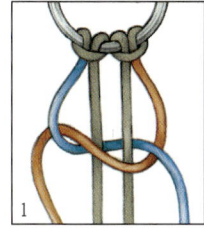

This creates a loop between each knotting cord and the core. Pass the rh cord through the loop on the left from front to back and the lh cord through the loop on the right from back to front.
2 Reverse the steps to make the second half of the knot: Cross the lh cord over the core and the rh cord under the core. Pass the lh cord through the loop on the right from front to back and the rh cord through the loop on the left from back to front.
3 Repeat steps 1 and 2 to the desired length to make a strong band of even width.

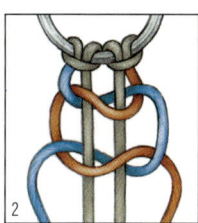

half knot
The half knot results in a twisted spiral. The photo below shows a series of half knots both with and without beads added. To make half knots, make the first half of a square knot, as in step 1 of "macramé square knot," at left. Repeat for the desired length, always crossing the right-hand knotting cord over the core and the left-hand knotting cord under the core. This will make your knots spiral to the left. If you want your knots to spiral to the right, cross the left-hand cord over the core and the right-hand cord under the core. If you wish, string a bead on each knotting cord between knots.

double half-hitch knot
Double half-hitch knots are formed by making two half-hitch knots around a core cord, also called a knot bearer. Place the knot bearer across the knotting cords at the specified angle. Wrap the first knotting cord around the core from front to back and go through the loop just formed under the knot bearer. Repeat, pulling it snug. The knot won't feel secure until the second knot is complete.

lark's head knot
1 Fold a cord in half and lay it behind the cord with the fold pointing up.
2 Bring the fold around the cord from back to front. Pull the ends through the fold and tighten.

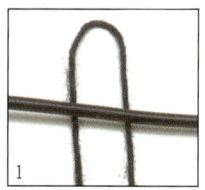 

overhand knot
Make a loop in the cord and bring the end that crosses on top behind the loop. Then pull it through to the front.

beaded backstitch
To stitch a line of beads, come up through the fabric from the wrong side. String three beads. Stretch the bead thread along the line where the beads will go, and go through the fabric right after the third bead. Come up through the fabric between the second and third beads and go through the third bead again. String three more beads and repeat. For a tighter stitch, string only two beads at a time.

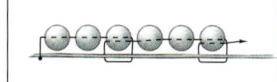

Bead & Button • Beaded Macramé Jewelry

Easy macramé clasp

All you need is two knots to make a clasp-free bracelet of one or many strands. To open the bracelet, just pull the ends apart on both sides of the macramé section that joins them. Tighten the bracelet by pulling the dangles to draw the strands against the macramé section.

❶ Measure your wrist; you'll string the number of beads it takes to achieve that length for each strand.

❷ For a four-strand bracelet as shown here, cut four 16-in. (41cm) lengths of nylon cord. Tie two strands together with an overhand knot (see "Basics," p. 3) 3 in. (7.6cm) or more from the end of the cords. Thread each cord onto a twisted wire needle. String both strands through one bead, and then string each cord with the number of beads needed to reach the length determined in step 1. String both strands through a final bead, and then tie the cords together against the beads with a square knot (see "Basics" and **photo a**). Do not trim the cords yet.

❸ Repeat step 2 with another pair of cords.

❹ Lay the beaded strands in a circle with the cord sections crossing. Tape or clip them together where they cross (**photo b**). There will be eight cords.

❺ Cut a 24-in. (61cm) length of nylon cord and center it under the crossed cords ½ in. (1.3cm) from one bead group. Tie the ends together around the cords. Then begin to work square knot macramé snugly around the bundle of cords (**photo c**) as shown in "Basics." Remove the tape or clip after making a few knots. When you have tied a section that is ½-¾ in. (1.3-1.9cm) long, pull the ends tight. To keep them from pulling out, cut them close and dab them with E6000 or cut them off, leaving about ¹⁄₁₆-in. (1.5mm) ends and singe them back to the knotted section with a lighter or match. Be careful not to melt the knots or strung cords.

❻ String a bead on a pair of strand ends. Tie an overhand knot to make a dangle that is 1-1½ in. (2.5-3.8cm) long (**photo d**). Trim the ends off close and singe back to the knot or dab it with glue. Repeat with the remaining six strands to make three more dangles. ●

– Louise Malcolm

materials

- **3 or more** strands (50 beads per strand) of 6 x 8mm faceted glass beads
- heavy nylon beading cord such as Conso, #5 or thicker (allow 16 in./41cm per strand, plus 24 in./61cm for the knots)
- twisted wire beading needle
- lighter or match or E6000 adhesive
- tape or paper clip

a

c

b

d

Beaded knots

Combine colorful cord with beads to make this easy necklace. Make it with square knots or use half knots to make the neckstraps spiral.

❶ Measure your neckline. Subtract the length of the button, the accent beads, and the focal bead. Divide by two to get the length of each neckstrap.

❷ Cut two 3-yd. (2.7m) lengths of waxed linen. Fold each cord 2 ft. (61cm) from one end and bring the folded portion of the cords through the shank of the button. With the 2-ft. lengths of cord between the 7-ft. (2.1m) sections, fasten each cord to the shank with a lark's head knot (see "Basics," p. 3 and **photo a**).

❸ Tie an inch (2.5cm) of square knots (see "Basics") around the pair of short ends (the core), using the long ones as the knotting cords (**photo b**).

❹ String a size 8º seed bead onto each knotting cord (**photo c**) and make a square knot (see "Basics"). Repeat until you reach the length determined in step 1. If you want your strap to spiral, use half knots rather than square knots.

❺ Slide one of the accent beads onto the core. Tie a square knot around the core on the other side of the bead (**photo d**) with the knotting cords.

❻ Slide the focal bead onto the core and make a square knot after it.

❼ Make the second side to match the first, but stop 1 in. from the end.

❽ To make a button loop, fold the core cords back toward the necklace, making a loop that's 1 in. long. Make two more knots over all four core cords (**photo e**). Even up the length of the loops and make square knots until the loop just fits over the button. Pull the last knot very tight and dot it with E6000 adhesive. Trim all the ends. ●
– Sibyl Rosen

a

c

e

b

d

materials
- focal bead
- **2** accent beads
- 2g size 6º or 8º seed beads
- 6 yd. (5.4m) waxed linen
- shank button
- E6000 adhesive

Elegant pearl choker

Make a statement when you suspend a beautiful mabé pearl pendant from a simply elegant band of knotted leather. If you don't want to use leather, there are alternative cords to choose from, such as silk, satin, or an imitation leather cord called P'leather.

Both sides of the choker are created separately beginning at the clasp using alternating square knots. Join the two sides in the middle through the tube beads and pearl pendant. Finish by adding accents on the cord ends.

alternating square knots

❶ To get your choker measurement, take the circumference of your neck, deduct the width of the pendant bail, beads, and clasp, and divide by 2. This result is the length of one half of your choker. For example, if your neck is 16 in. (41cm) and your beads, bail, and clasp come to 1½ in. (3.8cm), you need to have 7¼ in. (18.4cm) of macramé for each side of the choker.

Check the fit after you've completed the macramé sides. You can lengthen the choker or shorten it right before you secure it at the end.

❷ Attach two 2-yd. (1.8m) lengths of 1.5mm leather cord to the clasp. Pull both cords through the clasp and fold them in half. This gives you four working strands (**figure 1**). Secure the work to a macramé board with T-pins.

❸ The alternating square knot is tied on three cords instead of four to create a lace-like pattern. The first knot is tied on the left three cords, leaving the fourth cord hanging free. For the first half of the choker you will use the "RIGHT" square knot: Bring the right cord (cord 3) over the center cord (cord 2) and under the first cord (cord 1) (**photo a**). Take cord 1 under cord 2 and up through the loop that formed when cord 3 passed over the center cord (**photo b**). Take cord 1, which is now where cord 3 used to be, and go under cord two and over cord 3 (**photo c**). Cord 3 then goes over cord 2 and down through the new loop (**photo d**). Pull cords 1 and 3, making sure the knot is tight (**photo e**).

❹ For the next "row" use the right three cords, leaving the first cord (cord 1) hanging free. Repeat step 3 using cords 2, 3, and 4. There will be some free space above the knots that should be kept the same size in each row in order to achieve an even, lacy appearance (**figure 2**). Tie the next knot on the left three cords (cords 1, 2, and 3), leaving the fourth cord free again. Continue knotting, alternating between cords 1, 2, and 3, and cords 2, 3, and 4.

❺ The second half of the choker is created just like the first, except you use "LEFT" square knots. Attach the other two lengths of cord to the other end of the clasp to get your four working strands. This time, start with the right three cords (cords 2, 3, and 4), leaving cord 1 hanging free. Cord 2 goes over cord 3 and under cord 4. Cord 4 goes under cord 3 and up through the loop. Cord 4 passes under cord 3 again and over cord 2. Cord 2 goes over cord 3 and down through the loop. Repeat with cords 1, 2, and 3. Make the second half of the choker the same length as the first.

joining the sides

1 Slide a large-hole tube bead over all four cords on each side (**photo f**). Slide on the pendant and pull all of the cords through the pendant bail and the large-hole tube beads, giving you four strands of "whiskers" on each side (**photo g**).

2 Try on the choker for length and make sure it sits nicely on you. Pull the cords tighter or loosen them up a little. If they are too loose, it will hang like a necklace instead of a choker. If the bail is too loose, you can add extra cord through the beads and bail in the back.

3 Squirt some clear-drying glue such as E6000 inside the silver beads and pendant bail and let it dry. Arrange silver accent beads at various points on the "whiskers" and secure those with glue (**photo h**). It is easier to cut the extra cord after the beads have been placed and the glue is dry. ◐ – *Irina Serbina*

Email Irina at irina@macrameboutique.com or visit her website, macrameboutique.com.

tips

Symmetry

Since you want all your knots to face the same direction when the choker is worn, make "RIGHT" square knots, beginning with the right-hand knotting cord, and "LEFT" square knots beginning with the left-hand knotting cord.

materials

- mabé pearl pendant (macrameboutique.com)
- 2 large-hole silver tube beads
- 8 silver accent beads with 1.5mm opening
- 4 2-yd. (1.8m) lengths of 1.5mm leather cord
- silver clasp
- E6000 adhesive

Tools: macramé board (macrameboutique.com), T-pins

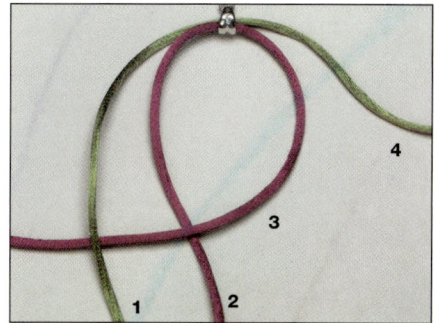
a

b

c

d

figure 1

cord 1 2 3 4

e

f

g

h

figure 2

Donut dangle

Dress up a stone donut with an embellished macramé dangle. This is a great project to try if you want to get acquainted with double half-hitch knots.

macramé embellishment

❶ Cut five 60-in. (1.5m) lengths of cord. Fold each cord in half and bring each loop up through the donut hole (**photo a**). Bring the ends of the cord through the loop and pull down, forming a lark's head knot (**photo b** and "Basics," p. 3).

❷ Working from left to right, number the cords 1–10. Separate cords 1–6 to the left and 7–10 to the right. Angle cord 6 over cords 5–1 (**photo c**). Working from right to left, make double half-hitch knots (see "Basics" and **figure 1**) starting with cord 5. Add a 5mm spacer before making the knot on cord 1.

❸ Angle cord 5 over cords 7–10. Working from left to right (**figure 2**), make double half-hitch knots starting with cord 7. Add a 5mm spacer before making the knot on cord 10. Your first row should look like **photo d**.

❹ Renumber the cords 1–10 so that the left-hand cord (which was #6) is now #1 and the right-hand cord (which was #5) is now #10. Repeat steps 2 and 3 without adding spacers on cords 1 and 10. Keep the rows snug against each other.

❺ To add center beads, string five spacers (two 4mm daisies, one 5mm spacer, two 4mm daisies) on cords 1 and 10, and string the rectangular bead on cords 5 and 6 (**photo e**). The rest of the cords will lie behind that bead.

❻ Angle cord 1 to the center below the rectangular bead over cords 2–5. Working left to right, make double half-hitch knots with cords 2–5.

❼ Renumber the cords 1-10 from left

8 Bead & Button • Beaded Macramé Jewelry

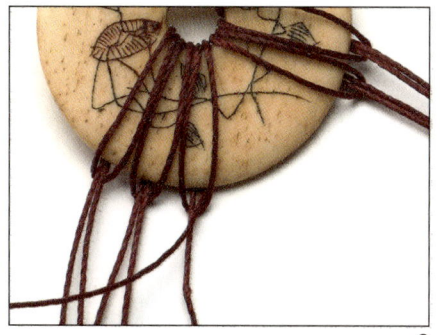

materials

- 40mm bone or stone donut
- 10mm Thai silver butterfly bead
- 20mm Thai silver diamond
- 4 5mm silver spacers
- 30 (approx.) 4mm daisy shaped spacers
- 10 (approx.) 1mm silver spacers
- assorted beads for dangles
- 3-in. (7.6cm) silver head pin
- 10mm twisted silver jump ring
- Conso beading cord, red
- 1 yd. (.9m) deerskin or suede cord

Tools: chainnose and roundnose pliers, lighter or match, wire cutters

Working R to L

figure 1

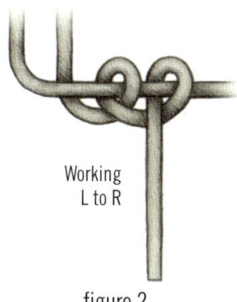

Working L to R

figure 2

Your piece should now look like **photo f**.
10 Renumber the cords. Place cord 1 over cords 2–5 and knot with cords 2–5.
11 Renumber the cords. Place cord 10 over cords 9–6 and knot with cords 9–6. The resulting buttonhole will hold the jump ring that attaches the silver butterfly (**photo g**). Repeat steps 10 and 11.
12 Renumber the cords. Place cord 1 over cords 2–5. Working left to right, knot with cords 2–5.
13 Renumber the cords. Place cord 10 over cords 9–5. Working right to left, knot with cords 9–5.
14 Repeat steps 6–9 to make two more complete rows below the buttonhole.

making the dangles

1 Stack a 1mm bead, 4mm daisy, silver butterfly, and a 4mm daisy on a head pin and make a wrapped loop (see "Making wrapped loops," p. 10) at the top.

to right. Angle cord 10 to the center over cords 9–5. Working right to left, knot with cords 9–5.
8 Renumber the cords. Place cord 1 over cords 2–6 and knot with cords 2–6.
9 Renumber the cords. Place cord 10 over cords 9–6 and knot with cords 9–6.

2 Open the jump ring (see "Opening jump rings," p. 10) and slide on the butterfly dangle. Put the jump ring through the buttonhole, capturing the bottom two macramé rows (**photo h**). Close the ring.
3 Bring cords 5 and 6 together beneath the jump ring and string a silver diamond and other desired components on both cords (**photo i**). This is the longest dangle. Make an overhand knot

Bead&Button • Beaded Macramé Jewelry

j

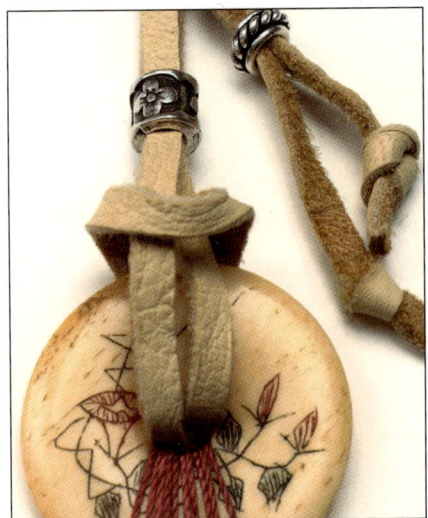
k

(see "Basics"), trim the tail, and singe the end with a lighter. Create ascending dangles on each side as desired.

❹ The daisy-shaped spacer on the front (**photo j**) is added last. Using the same cording, sew up from the back where you want the spacer to sit. String a spacer and a stop bead larger than the hole in the spacer. Go back through the spacer, tie off, trim the tail, and singe carefully.

❺ Secure a length of deerskin cord to the top of the donut with a lark's head knot and slide a silver bead over both cords (**photo k**). Add another silver stop bead near the ends and make an overhand knot at the end of each cord. ○
– Linnea Lockwood Gambino

Kits for this project are available for purchase. Contact Linnea by phone at (919) 345-4157 or email Linnayyah@aol.com and visit her website, Linnayyah.com.

tips

Making wrapped loops

Use wrapped loops to attach beads professionally and securely to your favorite jewelry.

❶ Make sure you have at least 1¼ in. (3.2cm) of wire above the bead. With the tip of your chainnose pliers, grasp the wire directly above the bead. Bend the wire (above the pliers) into a right angle.
❷ Using roundnose pliers, position the jaws vertically in the bend.
❸ Bring the wire over the top jaw of the roundnose pliers.
❹ Keep the jaws vertical and reposition the pliers' lower jaw snugly into the loop. Curve the wire downward around the bottom of the roundnose pliers. This is the first half of a wrapped loop.
❺ Position the chainnose pliers' jaws across the loop.
❻ Wrap the wire around the wire stem, covering the stem between the loop and the top bead. Trim the excess wire and press the cut end close to the wraps with chainnose pliers.

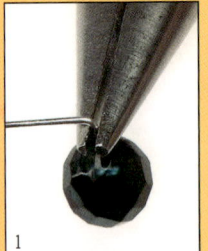
1

2

3

4

5

6

Opening jump rings

Because wire becomes work hardened with wear, try to manipulate it as little as possible.
❶ Hold the jump ring with two pairs of chainnose pliers or chainnose and roundnose pliers, as shown.
❷ To open the jump ring, bring the tips of one pair of pliers toward you and push the tips of the other pair away. String materials on the open jump ring. Reverse the steps to close it.

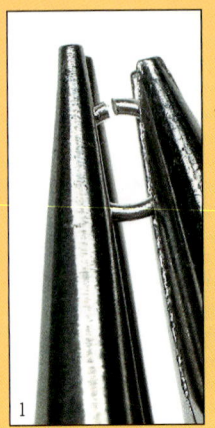
1
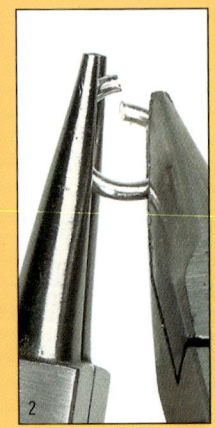
2

Embellished bracelet

Combine richly colored cord with Bali silver and gemstone beads to make an accessory you'll love. This complex-looking bracelet uses only three knots and is easier to make than it may appear. Use a macramé board with measured grid lines to help keep track of your progress and to hold the cord at a consistent angle. (As an alternative, tape graph paper to a corkboard or the cardboard core from a fabric bolt.) Start knotting at the button end of the bracelet. The instructions that follow make a bracelet that will fit a 7-in. (18cm) wrist.

If you have trouble stringing some of the beads, treat the last inch (2.5cm) or so of the cord with five-second nail glue. When the glue is dry, cut the end of the cord at a steep angle. The glue turns the cord into its own needle.

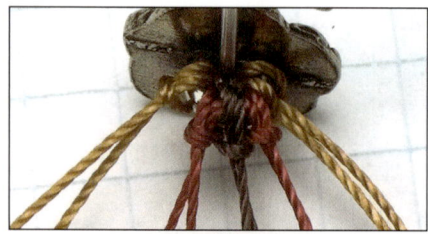
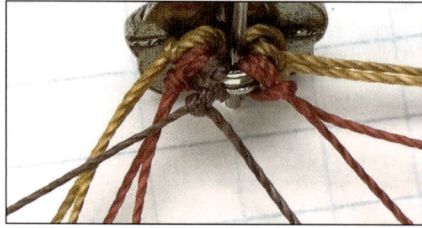
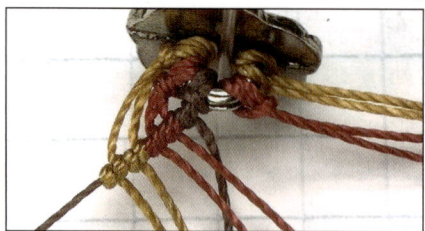
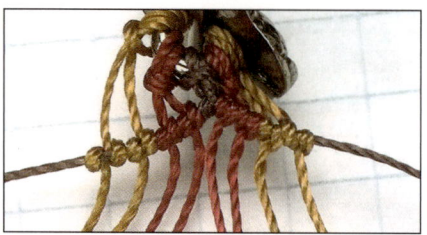

getting started

❶ Cut two 1-yd. (.9m) lengths of the light and medium cords and one of the dark cord.

❷ Tie each cord to the shank of the button with a lark's head knot (see "Basics," p. 3) so the ends are even. You'll have ten half-yard cords. Position them on the button as follows: light, medium, dark, medium, and light. Attach the button to the knotting board with a T-pin (**photo a**).

❸ Number the cords 1-10 from left to right. Set cords 7-10 aside with a T-pin.

❹ Use cord 6 (dark) for the first series of knots. Place cord 6 over cords 5-1 at a 45-degree angle (this is the knot bearer). Make a double half-hitch knot around it with cord 5 (see "Basics" and **photo b**). Repeat this step, tying a double half-hitch around the same bearing cord with each subsequent cord to the left. Hold the bearing cord under tension at the angle in the direction that you want the knots to form. This will produce an angled chevron pattern with the center knot further back than the edge knot. This is row 1 (**photo c**).

❺ Renumber the cords 1-10 from left to right so that the left-hand cord (which was #6) is now #1. Pin cords 1-5 out of the way. Place cord 6 over cords 7-10 at a 45-degree angle and make double half-hitch knots from left to right starting with cord 7 (**photo d**).

❻ Repeat steps 4 and 5 until you have knotted eight rows on each side (the light cords will be in the center—**photo e**). For a wrist that's smaller or larger than 7 in., adjust the number of rows in this and the corresponding end section.

beading the side section

The two center cords will always be the same color when you add beads.

❶ String a square Bali bead on the two middle (light) cords. String a small Bali spacer on each of the edge cords (**photo f**). Slide the beads snugly against the knotting.

❷ Renumber the cords 1-10 from left to right. Pin right below the small Bali spacer on cord 1 to to hold the bead in place. Angle cord 1 over cords 2-5 and tie double half-hitch knots around it with each cord, until you reach the center. Repeat on the other side, angling cord 10 over cords 9-5 and making double half-hitch knots toward the center (**photo g**).

❸ Renumber the cords 1-10 from left to right. Angle cord 10 over cords 9-6 and make double half-hitch knots from right to left. Renumber the cords 1-10 again. Angle cord 1 over cords 2-8 and make double half-hitch knots from left to right.

❹ Before completing the last two knots, string a daisy spacer, a 6º seed bead, and a daisy on the next-to-last cord. String a 4mm stone, a dangle, and a stone on the last cord (**photo h**). Push the beads up snugly and finish knotting with cords 9 and 10 to the right (**photo i**).

❺ Renumber the cords 1-10. To complete the X pattern, set cords 6-10 aside. Angle cord 5 over cords 4-3 and make double half-hitch knots from right to left. String beads on cords 1 and 2 as in step 4. Finish knotting to the left on cords 2 and 1 (**photo j**). Complete the section by adding a second row of knots below the first. This completes the first section of the bracelet.

❻ Repeat steps 1-3 of "beading the side section." Substitute the following beads in step 1: on the edge cords string a 6º, a daisy, a stone, a daisy, and a 6º. On the center pair of cords, string a small Bali spacer, a 6mm fire-polished bead, and a small Bali spacer.

❼ Repeat steps 4-5 of "beading the side section," substituting the following beads: On the edge cord string a 2mm silver hex, a stone bead, a dangle, a stone, and a hex. On the next-to-last cord string only a small Bali spacer.

❽ Repeat steps 1-3, stringing a small Bali spacer on the edge cords. On the center pair of cords, string a large oval Bali bead.

❾ Repeat steps 4-5. String a small Bali spacer on the next-to-last cord. On the edge cord, string a 6º, a daisy, a stone, a daisy, and a 6º.

knotting the center and second half

The center is a bit time-consuming. Be patient so you get the alignment right.

❶ Renumber the cords 1-10. On cord 1 (medium color), string a 1.5mm bead, daisy, stone, daisy, garnet pendant, daisy, stone, daisy, and 1.5mm bead.

Thread cords 2 and 3 (medium and dark) together through a small Bali spacer, the end hole of the spacer bar, and a small Bali spacer. Cord 4 (light) lies below the spacer bar. Thread cords 5 and 6 (light) through a star spacer, stone rondelle, star spacer, the center hole of the spacer bar, star spacer, stone rondelle, and star spacer. Cord 7 (light) lies below the spacer bar. String cords 8 and 9 like cords 2 and 3. String cord 10 (medium) through a 1.5mm bead, daisy, stone, daisy, dangle, daisy, stone, daisy, and a 1.5mm bead (**photo k**).

❷ With the beads strung, resume knotting, being sure to snug up the beads as you go and maintain the color order that has been established. Knot as in steps 2-3 of "beading the side section."

❸ Repeat steps 9 then 8 of the side section exactly.

❹ Repeat steps 7 then 6 exactly.

❺ Repeat steps 4-5 exactly. Then repeat steps 1-2.

❻ Continue knotting toward the center, angling cord 1 over cords 2-5 and cord 10 over cords 9-5. Make as many additional rows of double half-hitch knots in this manner as needed to match the number of rows established in step 6 of "getting started."

making the buttonhole

❶ Renumber the cords 1-10 from left to right.

❷ Use cords 6 and 10 to make square knots (see "Basics" and **figure**) over cords 7-9 until the side is long enough to accommodate the button (**photo l**).

❸ Repeat step 2 on the left-hand side, using cords 1 and 5 to knot over cords 2-4. Work the same number of knots on each side.

❹ Renumber the cords 1-10 from left to right. Join the two sides together by making a square knot with cords 4 and 7 over cords 5 and 6.

❺ Angle cord 10 over cords 9-6 and tie double half-hitch knots from right to left. Renumber the cords 1-10 from left to right. Angle cord 1 over cords 2-6 and make double half-hitch knots toward the center, forming a V.

❻ Repeat step 5 so two rows secure the buttonhole (**photo m**).

materials

- 2 yd. (1.8m) each **3 colors** Conso, bonded jewelry twine or #8 nylon bead cord (light, medium, and dark)

Bali silver beads:
- three-hole spacer
- **2** 8-10mm oval silver beads
- **2** 6-7mm square beads
- **4** 5-7mm flat star spacers
- **8** 2mm silver hex beads
- **9** daisy flower dangles or other dangles
- **24** 3-4mm spacers
- **30** 4-5mm flat daisy spacers

Other beads
- garnet pendant, 14-20mm long
- **2** 6-8mm fire-polished beads
- **2** 5-8mm rondelles
- **4** 1.5mm silver beads
- **20** size 6º seed beads
- **28** 4mm garnet beads
- decorative shank button

Tools: macramé board (available on Linnea's website), T-pins, lighter or match

Optional: 5-second nail glue

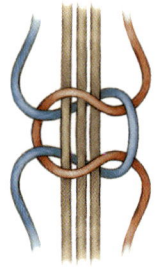

❼ Cut the cords ¹⁄₁₆ in. (1.5mm) from the last row of knots.

❽ Singe the end of each cord, sealing the knots. Hold the flame below and to the side of each tail until it starts to shrivel into a ball. Be careful not to get it too close or the ball will turn black. ●

– Linnea Lockwood Gambino

Contact Linnea by phone (919) 345-4157 or email Linnayyah@aol.com and visit her website, Linnayyah.com.

h

i

j

k

l

m

Hippie chic choker

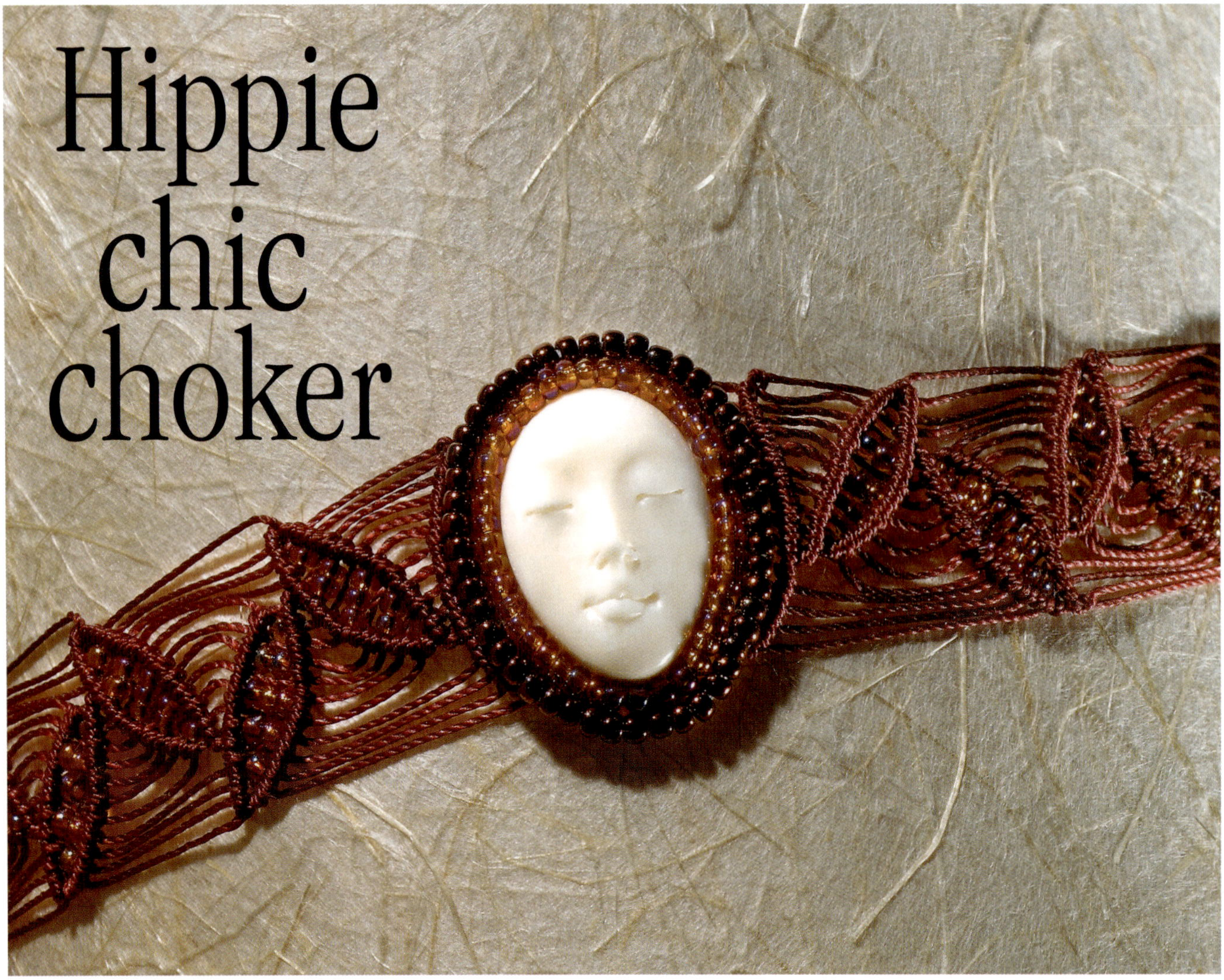

Macramé is often associated with bold colors and textures, but it can also be soft and sinuous. By using fine cord that comes in an array of beautiful colors, you can create delicate pieces that look like they're floating on air.

Create a beaded bezel for the cabochon, then measure, cut, and attach the cords. Knot the first side, finishing it with a strip of square knots. Knot the other side to match the first, but finish with a beaded loop. Use double half-hitch knots for your horizontal and diagonal lines and square knots to make the ends.

beaded bezel

❶ Glue a cabochon to a piece of Ultrasuede with E6000 adhesive. Remove excess glue from around the edges.
❷ Thread a needle with 1 yd. (.9m) of Nymo and tie an overhand knot (see "Basics," p. 3) at the end. Bring the needle up through the Ultrasuede close to the cab. Using size 11º or 8º seed beads, backstitch (see "Basics") around the cab, ending with an even number of beads (**photo a**).
❸ Once the cab is encircled, begin even-count circular peyote (see "Even-count circular peyote," p. 15) from the base row. When you get all the way around the cab, step up (**photo b**) to start the next row. Add enough rows to secure the cab.
❹ The cab component must be at least 1 in. (2.5cm) from top to bottom to cover all the cords. Trim the Ultrasuede close to the beads without cutting your

a

b

beadwork. Cut an identical piece of Ultrasuede to cover the back.

5 Cut 16 80-in. (2m) lengths of cord (this makes a 16-in./41cm choker). Lay them out horizontally side by side and mark the middle.

6 Apply a thin, even layer of E6000 to the back of the beaded cab and glue it over the cords at the mark. Keep the cords flat.

7 Flip the cab over, keeping all the cords in order. Apply E6000 to the second piece of Ultrasuede and glue it to the back of the cab, covering all the cords evenly (**photo c**). Let it dry.

knot the leaves (side one)

Anchor the cab vertically to a macramé board with T-pins to keep it flat and stabilized. If you don't have a macramé board, devise a work surface that will hold your piece in place.

1 Lay cord 1 across the other cords, keeping it against the cab (**figure 1**).

2 Starting with cord 2, make double half-hitch knots around cord 1 all the way across, keeping cord 1 in line with the cab (**figure 2** and **photo d**).

3 Renumber the cords 1-16 from left to right so that the left-hand cord (which was #2) is now #1 and the right-hand cord (which was #1) is #16. Set cords 1-4 aside with a T-pin. Angle cord 5 over cords 6-16. Starting with cord 6, make double half-hitch knots with each cord around cord 5, working left to right. This is the top border of the first leaf.

4 Using size 11º or 8º seed beads, string one on cord 7, two on cord 9, three on cord 11, two on cord 13, and one on cord 15.

5 Snug the beads up to the border of the leaf and lay cord 6 across the bottom (**photo e**). Starting with cord 7, make double half-hitch knots around cord 6 working left to right to the end, keeping the bottom border snug to the beads. This completes the first leaf.

6 Renumber the cords 1-16 from left to right and set cords 13-16 aside with a T-pin.

7 Lay cord 12 diagonally across cords 11-1. Starting with cord 11, make double half-hitch knots around cord 12, working right to left (**photo f**).

8 String one bead on cord 10, two on

c

d

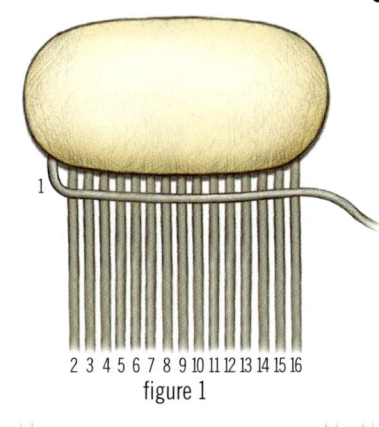

2 3 4 5 6 7 8 9 10 11 12 13 14 15 16
figure 1

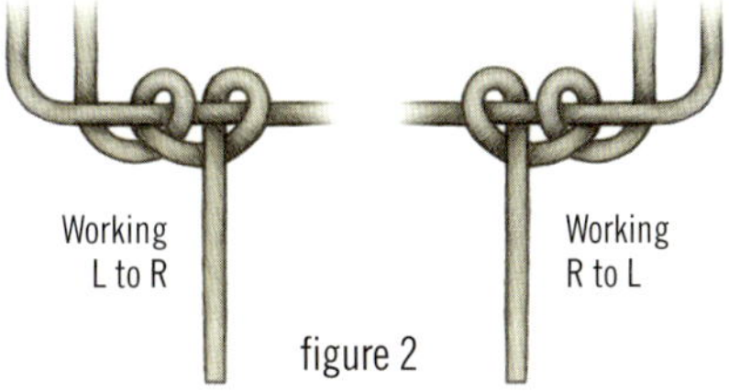

Working L to R   Working R to L

figure 2

e

f

tip

Even-count circular peyote

To make a beautiful centerpiece, secure a cabochon to Ultrasuede using even-count circular peyote stitch.

1 Exit a bead on the backstitched ring. Pick up a bead, skip a bead on the ring, and go through the next bead. Repeat around the cabochon in this manner until you're back to the start. Because the beads nestle together in peyote stitch, you now have three rows.

2 Since you started with an even number of beads, you need to work a step up to be in position for the next row. Go through the last bead in row 2 (the numbers in the illustration indicate rows) and the first bead in row 3. Pick up a bead and go through the second bead of row 3; continue.

3 Decrease, if necessary, to tighten the stitches around the cabochon. To decrease, pick up a bead as usual and go through the next two beads instead of just one.

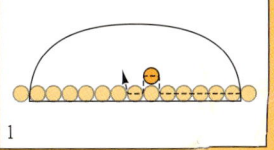

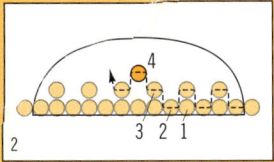

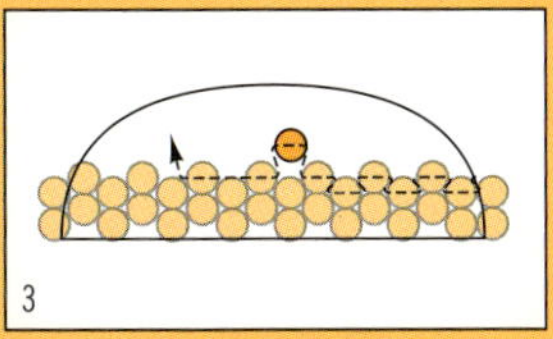

Bead & Button • Beaded Macramé Jewelry   15

g

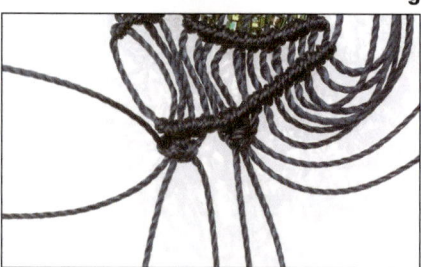
h

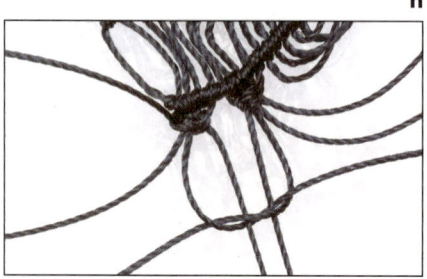
i

j

k

l

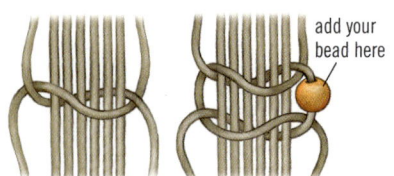
figure 3

cord 8, three on cord 6, two on cord 2, and one on cord 1. Snug the beads up and lay cord 11 across the bottom.
❾ Starting with cord 10, make double half-hitch knots around cord 11 working right to left all the way to the end.
❿ Repeat steps 3-9 until you have made 18 leaves.

making the ends
❶ After the last leaf, renumber the cords 1-16 from left to right. Lay cord 1 horizontally over all the cords and make a row of double half-hitch knots straight across, working from left to right.
❷ Make a bed of alternating square knots (see "Basics") to support the button (**photo g**): Starting from the left, make a square knot with cords 2, 3, 4, and 5. For the first half of the knot, cord 2 goes under 3 and 4. Cord 5 goes under 2, over 3 and 4, and down through the loop made by 2. To complete the knot, cord 5 goes over 3 and 4; 2 goes over 5, under 3 and 4, and down through the loop made by 5.
❸ Make another knot next to it with cords 6, 7, 8, and 9 (**photo h**). Join the two sections together by making the next knot with cords 4, 5, 6, and 7 (**photo i**).

❹ Continue making square knots and connecting the sections all the way across until you've made a 1-in. (2.5cm) long section. Lay cord 2 horizontally over all the cords and make a row of double half-hitch knots straight across.
❺ Renumber the cords 1-16 from left to right and set aside cords 9-16. Working from the left, string one 8º or 11º bead on cord 3, two on cord 5, and three on cord 7. Use cord 1 as a bearing cord and tie double half-hitch knots across to the center, snugging up the beads. Repeat on the right side with one bead on cord 14, two beads on cord 12, and three on cord 10. Use cord 16 as a bearing cord and make double half-hitch knots toward the center (**photo j**).
❻ Knot the bearing cords together at the center with a square knot. Cut the cords close to the knots and dot with G-S Hypo Cement.

knot the leaves (side two)
❶ Repeat steps 1-10 of "knot the leaves (side one)."
❷ Make one to three more rows of horizontal double half-hitch knots (**photo k**). Do not cut the cords. Try on the choker to see if it fits.

materials
16-in. (41cm) choker
- 20mm (approx.) cabochon (Rio Grande, riogrande.com)
- 5g size 11º or 8º seed beads
- 4 x 4-in. (10 x 10cm) piece of Ultrasuede (available from fabric stores)
- Nymo B beading thread
- beeswax or Thread Heaven
- beading needles, # 12
- 35 yd. (32m) Tuff Cord, size 3 (Shor International, shorinternational.com)
- shank button
- E6000 adhesive
- G-S Hypo Cement

Tools: macramé board, T-pins

Size adjustment can be made with placement of the button or by adding more double half-hitch rows here.
❸ To make the beaded loop (**photo l**), divide the 16 cords into two sections. Starting with the eight-cord section on the right, make seven beaded square knots, working the two outer cords over six inner cords. String a seed bead on the exterior cord of each square knot (**figure 3**).
❹ Work the left eight-cord section to mirror the right, keeping the beads on the outermost cords. Seven to nine knots will allow a ⅝-in. (1.6cm) button to pass through. Make more knots if your button is bigger.
❺ Tie the two sections together with a large square knot by working the two outermost cords over 14 inner cords. Cut the cords and dot with G-S Hypo Cement.
❻ Sew a button to the bed of square knots on the other side. ●

– Annika deGroot

Visit Annika's website, annikadegroot.com or email her at jofre146@juno.com.

Thunderbird choker

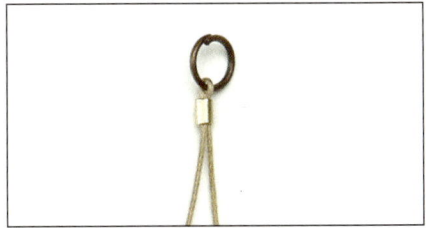
a

b

c

d

Including beads in a macramé project can be challenging if the bead holes are too small, as is often the case with gemstone beads. This clever design sidesteps that potential problem by incorporating a strand of flexible beading wire onto which beads are strung. Beaded dangles strung on head pins provide additional pizzazz.

getting started

❶ Cut one 2-yd. (1.8m) length of each color of waxed linen (two each of cream and gold), plus one 18-in. (46cm) piece of dark blue. Cut 18 in. of flexible beading wire and crimp one end of it to a jump ring (see "Basics," p. 3 and **photo a**).

❷ Gather all the cords except the 18-in. dark blue one together and, leaving a 3-in. group tail, wrap them around the jump ring. Wrap the 18-in. dark blue strand tightly around all the cords and the beading wire a few times. Continue wrapping the blue linen around the group of cords and the jump ring until you have formed a small ring (**photo b**).

❸ Wrap very loosely around the entire group of doubled cords below the ring (including the tail of the dark blue strand you are using) four or five times. Insert the leading end of the dark blue cord through the loosely wrapped portion (**photo c**) and tug and adjust until you have tightened the wraps around the entire group of doubled cords and both dark blue tails. Clip all tails (**photo d**).

begin the neckstrap

The first portion of the neckstrap is made up of five sets of square knots, each set using a different pair of colors for the knotting cords. Use the following color combinations, as shown here, or choose your own.

1. off-white and turquoise
2. coral and gold
3. dark blue and yellow
4. gold and light blue
5. turquoise and coral

Use the rest of the cords and the wire as your anchor.

❶ Skip down about ½ in. (1.3cm) from the knotted loop and work three square knots (see "Basics") with the first set of knotting cords. *Skip down ½ in. and make three square knots with the next set of cords*. Repeat from * to * three more times (**photo e**, p. 18).

❷ Repeat from * to * one more time, using dark blue and gold for your knotting cords, and arranging all the cords so that they emerge from the last group of square knots in the

Bead & Button • Beaded Macramé Jewelry

17

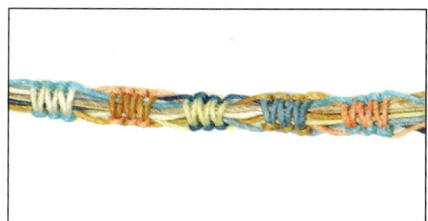

e

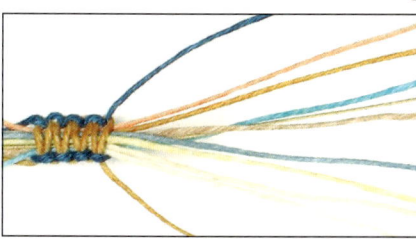

f

g

h

following order from bottom to top: gold, cream, cream, yellow, light blue, beige, turquoise, gold, coral, and dark blue (**photo f**).

❸ Drop the wire for the time being—just let it hang loose. Using the bottom gold cord as your anchor, work a double half-hitch knot (see "Basics") with each color of cord from bottom to top at a slight angle (**photo g**). Each successive cord along the top edge of your work will be a bit longer than the last and the cords will form a "floating" arc with dark blue at the top.

❹ Using the bottom cream cord as your anchor cord, work double half-hitch knots with each color as before, leaving a tiny space between this row of knots and the previous one but placing the two rows closer and closer as you work your way upwards. End with the dark blue cord (**photo h**). Do not knot with the final gold cord—just leave it hanging for now. This double half-hitch should rest snugly up against

tip

Waxed linen

When waxed linen is knotted tightly, the wax causes the cords to adhere to one another, making adhesives unnecessary.

the one in the previous row of knots.
❺ Repeat step 4 twice, first using the second cream cord as your anchor cord and omitting the cream cord at the top. and then using the yellow cord as your anchor cord and omitting the second cream cord at the top.
❻ Repeat again, using the light blue cord as your anchor cord and omitting the yellow cord at the top. Before you make your last double half-hitch knot with the dark blue cord, join the wire with the light blue cord as part of your anchor (**photo i**).
❼ Drop the wire again for the time being and set it aside with the gold, two cream, and yellow cords that were omitted in steps 4-6. Make four more rows of double half-hitch knots, using the bottom cord (beige first, turquoise second, gold third, and coral fourth) as your anchor. Do not omit the top cord on these rows, except on the last repeat.
❽ Pick up the four cords you set aside in step 7 (gold, two cream, and yellow) and, using the two cream cords as your anchor, work three square knots with the gold and yellow cords (**photo j**).
❾ On the wire, string a daisy spacer, a gold spacer, a lapis bead, a spacer, and one more daisy spacer.
❿ Wrap the coral cord once all the way around the wire after the beads just strung, and then back up to the top of your work. Leave it hanging there for now. Wrap the bottom gold cord once around the wire at the same spot and back down towards the bottom half of your work (**photo k**). Leave the wire hanging free for now.
⓫ Working along the bottom of the

piece, use the light blue, beige, and turquoise cords as your anchor and work 12 half knots (see "Basics") with gold and dark blue (**photo l**). As you finish the last few half knots, make sure that your anchor cords emerge in the following order from bottom to top: turquoise, beige, light blue.
⓬ Working along the top of the piece, use the yellow and two cream cords as your anchor and work eight square knots with gold and coral.
⓭ On the wire, string a daisy spacer, a gold spacer, a turquoise bead, a coral bead (substitute coral-colored glass beads, if desired), a turquoise bead, a gold spacer, and a daisy spacer.
⓮ Using the coral cord from the top of your work and the dark blue cord from the bottom, work one-and-one-half square knots around the beading wire after the beads just strung.
⓯ Working along the top of the piece, and using the yellow and two cream cords as your anchor, work five square knots with dark blue and gold. This takes you to the top center of the piece.
⓰ Working along the bottom of the piece, and using the gold cord as your anchor, work a double half-hitch knot with each color from bottom to top at an angle. Leave a little space between rows at the bottom, decreasing that space as you work upwards. Repeat four more times, using turquoise as your next your anchor, then beige, then light blue, then coral. This brings you to the bottom center of the piece.

beading the center section
On the wire, string a lapis bead, a daisy spacer, a gold spacer, a tiger jasper bead (here, a topaz-colored glass bead), a gold spacer, a daisy spacer, and a lapis bead (**photo m**).

working the second side
Make the second half of the choker by repeating what you've just done in reverse.
❶ Working along the bottom of the piece, make five rows of double half-hitch knots from top to bottom. For symmetry, angle your rows in the opposite direction of those on the first side. Increase the space between rows as you work your way downward. Begin

with coral as your anchor, then light blue, beige, turquoise, and finally gold.
❷ Working along the top of the piece, and using the yellow and two cream cords as your anchor, work five square knots with the dark blue and gold cords.
❸ Using the coral cord from the top of your work and the dark blue cord from the bottom, work one-and-one-half square knots around the flexible beading wire.
❹ Working along the top of the piece, use the yellow and two cream cords as your anchor and work eight square knots with gold and coral.
❺ Working along the bottom of the piece, use the light blue, beige, and turquoise cords as your anchor and work 12 half knots with the gold and dark blue cords.
❻ On the wire, string a daisy spacer, a gold spacer, a turquoise bead, a coral bead, a turquoise bead, a gold spacer, and a daisy spacer.
❼ Wrap the coral cord once all the way around the wire after the beads and spacers just strung, and down to the bottom of your work. Leave it hanging there for now. Wrap the bottom gold cord once around the wire at the same spot and back down towards the bottom half of your work. Leave the wire hanging free for now.
❽ You should now have a gold cord, two cream cords, one yellow cord, and the wire hanging loose at the top of your work. Using the two cream cords as your anchor (and leaving the wire aside), work three square knots with the gold and yellow cords.
❾ Working along the bottom of the piece, start working your rows of double half-hitch knots from top to bottom, angling your rows appropriately for symmetry, and increasing the distance between rows as you work your way downward. Begin with coral as your anchor, then gold, turquoise, beige, and then light blue.
❿ On the wire, string a daisy spacer, a gold spacer, a lapis bead, a spacer, and one more daisy spacer.
⓫ Join the wire with your yellow cord as anchor cord for the first double half-hitch only of the next row of double half-hitch knots. Leave the wire hanging. Continue your rows of double half-hitch knots, using first yellow as your anchor cord, then cream, cream again, and finally gold.

finish the neckstrap
❶ Arrange the cords as the emerge from the last row of double half-hitch knots so they form a small floating arc with dark blue at the top. Make five sets of square knots so the second neckstrap is the mirror image of the first.
❷ Gather all your cords except the dark blue one together and wrap the group around a jump ring, leaving about ¾ in. (1.9cm) space before the ring. Crimp the beading wire to the ring in the middle of the group of cords. Hold all the cords together to form a loop around the jump ring. Using the dark blue cord, wrap as in step 2 of "getting started." Clip all tails.

complete the choker
❶ Open a jump ring (see "Opening jump rings," p. 10) and slide it onto one of the cord-wrapped loops. Repeat on the other side. String a clasp on one jump ring and an extender chain on the other, if desired. Close the jump rings.
❷ String beads on head pins as shown in **photo n** and make the first half of a wrapped loop (see "Making wrapped loops," p. 10) at the top of each.

materials
- Irish waxed linen (4-ply) in the following colors and lengths:
    2 yd. (1.8m) each of light blue, turquoise, yellow, coral, and beige
    2.5 yd. (2.3m) of dark blue
    4 yd. (3.6m) of gold and cream,
- **2** 4 x l2mm tiger jasper or tiger eye
- **7** 4 x 6mm coral beads
- **11** 4mm round turquoise beads
- **15** 4mm round lapis lazuli
- **34** copper 4mm daisy spacers
- **34** flat gold 4mm spacers
- flexible beading wire, .014-.015
- **2** gold crimp beads
- hook and eye clasp
- **9** gold or copper head pins
- **4** 8mm jump rings

Tools: macramé board, T-pins, wire cutters, roundnose and chainnose pliers
Optional: 6-in. (15cm) extender chain, crimping pliers

i

j

k

l

m

n

Connect them to the bottom of the necklace, as shown on p. 17, and complete the wraps. ○
– *Melody MacDuffee*

Contact Melody at writersink@msn.com.

Get Great Jewelry Projects All Through the Year!

Your Beading Resource!

Bead&Button magazine
- New and traditional stitching techniques
- Fully-tested projects
- Step-by-step instructions and photos

Fast. Fashionable. Fun.

BeadStyle magazine
- Beautiful pieces in today's hottest styles
- Make jewelry in an evening or less
- Great photos and easy-to-follow instructions

If you enjoyed *Beaded Macramé Jewelry*, make sure you order these titles from the Easy-Does-It Series.

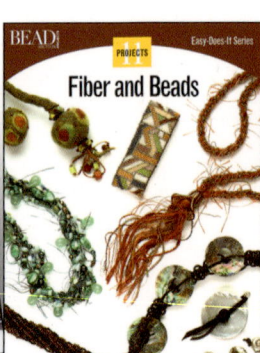
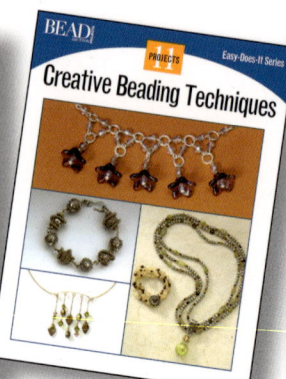

Subscribe or Order Today and Enjoy New Beading Projects Every Month! Call 800-533-6644 or visit beadandbuttonbooks.com

ISBN 0-89024-463-4 $7.95 U.S. 12285